Acknowledgement

I would like to thank my son Munashe for helping me with typing my work. It did make such a big difference. To Mrs. Alice Marecha, Mr. Kudzai Marecha, Ms. Teresa Ndiweni, Anne Gwanzura and Ms. Anastacia Mutsauri, thank you very much for the encouragement. Its people like you who make things happen and finally to Mrs. Abigail Tagwireyi, its those critics which motivated me. I do appreciate you all. Thank you.

THE BLAZE THAT DESTROYED MY SHADOW

Chapter 1

Family Background

Having grown up in the South, I never thought that I would ever move out of the province where I was born. I love my sunshine and honestly, I never dreamt that I would ever relocate up North. Yes, visiting was never a big issue as I would be guaranteed to come back home where I enjoy my short winters and my beautiful weather.

My friends always teased me that I would never give up my sunshine for anything. That's the worst thing I would ever do to myself. I remember when I was a kid every once in a while we would visit my mother's sister who lived in Calgary. I must say the only time I appreciated going there was during Christmas holidays. This was because even if I was in Toronto, which is my hometown where I was born and grew up, it would also be the time that it would probably be snowing as well. It was also a normal thing that every kid loved the white Christmas. If it didn't snow, it wouldn't be considered a great Christmas. Christmas time was the only time I used to like building a Mr. Snowman with my friends outside otherwise any other times I never liked to play outside.

My mother always said that I wasn't a normal kid for my age. Unlike my siblings who would only come in the house if my parents called them. I would always come up with every excuse to make sure that I never go and play outside during winter. They ended up giving up on me and I only did some indoor activities.

My brother Sam and my sister Shanna were on hockey teams. I just couldn't stand the cold so I chose sports like football and swimming. I loved swimming and I always competed for my junior team at my school. My friends always called me a fish when it came to swimming because I always came first during competitions. This was my best hobby as well.

My father liked involving me when he was doing activities like gardening at home. I loved cutting grass so much that most of the summer seasons my family knew they had a garden boy. That is to just give you an idea of how much I love warm weather.

My best moments as a kid were when we took those out of Canada vacations in winter. We usually went to Jamaica or Mexico. I loved those moments.

My name is Shelton and I grew up in a family of three. Sam is the eldest and I'm in the middle then

Shanna. There is always this thing about being a middle child, I felt like my brother and sister always got what they wanted on time and I was just floating in there.

I found out that If I asked for anything from my dad, he would give me a big lecture first before saying yes. Same with my mom, she would preach and tell me how I'm different from my siblings because they always did what she asked. I didn't understand why I was being treated otherwise but as I grew older I realized that usually during the winter times my brother liked helping with shovelling the snow while I stayed inside. They all called me hot headed.

Besides that, I had a wonderful family. I always got all the support I needed and my father being a chemist, failing at school was a no-no to him. That man loved sciences and when it came to our school, he made sure that we always came out on top. That's how I was always on the honour roll most of the time. He always said that he will raise doctors. That was his wish for all of us but if only wishes were horses, beggars would ride. Out of the three of us, he raised one doctor. Oncologist Doctor Sam Peters. Sam made us proud. He was a genius. I always told him that he had the natural intelligence which was unlike myself. I had to study hard for my grades. Nothing came easily. Shanna was also very intelligent and she ended up being a pharmacist so you can actually see that science ran in our blood.

Choosing a career for me was one of the toughest things I have ever done. Although I thought I knew my capabilities, my father, Doug Peters was aiming higher than I could imagine. I knew he was only trying to be the best father but he didn't realize that I was different from Sam. I wanted something technical. That was my passion and to be honest I sat down with my friends and we decided together. Our prayers and wishes were to be enrolled at the same college and do the same program. You know how it is when you are teenagers. We were a group of three, Tim, Jimmy and I.

When it came to the time to apply for college, we sat together and filled our forms the same. We chose the same programs and the same schools. At the end of two weeks we got conditional acceptance letters at Mohawk College. We only needed to pass our end of term exams and our places would be secured. We were all going to enrol for oil and gas engineering which was a three-year program.

At the end of the semester we all passed with flying colours and our places now became confirmed. My father supported me even though he had wanted me to go into the medical field. He mentioned that we don't always get what we want in this life but he was happy that I was starting on a great career. That summer holiday was one of the best for me and my friends. We got work at Canada's Wonderland and it was busy and fun at the same time.

When school opened in September, we went to stay closer to our college which was located in Hamilton. I had an option of staying at home and commuting but I was concerned about the distance especially during winter months. I didn't want to take any chances so we ended up renting a three-bedroom apartment which the three of us shared. My fear was to go and live with strangers so it worked out well when we got the apartment. It is always hard to get out of your comfort zone so it worked out well.

School was a challenge but we worked very hard to maintain our grades and goals. We were always on the top. Since we were also in the same program, it made life much easier for us since we always studied and did our homework together. It worked out very well.

Most weekends I would go home and spend time with my parents. The distance made our relationship stronger. My dad would call or text a couple of times a day, and talking of my mother, it was like we lived on different continents. She wanted to know what I was wearing, what I ate for breakfast, how my school was and if I had enough food etc. When I left home on Sundays for school my mother made sure that she cooked my meals for the whole week and like someone who enjoyed baking, every week I brought a different type of cake. Sam was far from home. Carlton University was about five hours drive and he told our parents that he did not want so many visits because his program was very challenging so he needed to spend more time on his books. That was most expected. Medicine was not a joke at all.

I believe my parents were beginning to feel lonely, with my sister never at home, they were left with me only and I did enjoy that. I got to get the best treatment I wanted.

Shanna was also finishing high school the same year and she was working harder to get enrolled for her Bachelor of Pharmacy Degree. Besides her studies, she also had this fashion thing which my dad said he couldn't cope with. Shanna loved herself and she was always up to date with her hair dos, make up and her designer clothing and shoes. All her stuff were labels, that's why she had to work harder to keep up. My parents were not bothered as long as she was on top with her school.

At one point I felt like I was the baby of the house, like those times I would be home with my parents alone. My mother stated that she wouldn't know how it would feel like when Shanna left them for university. Shanna wanted to be as far away from home as possible hence they were going to be left with only myself closer to them. Once in a while I would tease them that I wanted to transfer to a college further away and my mother would freak out.

Those were just mere words I used to scare her. The truth was, I didn't even know how Sam did it because I could never imagine myself away from my family. I was so much attached to my mother and I knew how to get what I wanted from her. My mother chose the best career because as a Registered Nurse she had the softest heart ever. She always pampered us.

This wonderful mother of mine was a lady full of love and integrity. She taught us values and through her I learnt to be respectful. She always reminded us never to take advantage of anyone especially the less privileged.

My mother was a beautiful woman both inside and outside. She was also of a strong personality. From what I learnt from her, she was given away for adoption just after birth. She had a twin sister and they were both adopted by the same family. She always appreciated the parents who raised her and said she couldn't imagine how her life could have turned out if not for them. The most important thing that she appreciated was that she grew up together with her sister and the two were best friends. Their parents didn't have any other children except the two.

She always mentioned how my dad never took advantage of her and she wanted us to be the same. These were some of the statements that had great significance in our lives. I felt so blessed to be a son to such a wonderful couple because my dad was no exception. I know my friends always admired me for having such a supportive father like mine. I love my parents.

My siblings were always there for me as well. In fact, we were very supportive of each other and we made most life decisions together. We did most activities together especially during the holidays and this glued us together. Not having mentioned that my grandparents on my mother's side were also pastors at a local church, so you could imagine my mother. She would always call us to pray. She always mentioned that a family that prays together stays together. It did work with our family.

Chapter 2

Graduation

Time flies, three years were done in no time. Before you know it, it was time to graduate. I graduated with first class Honours. All my family members were there to celebrate this happy moment with me. I must confess, this was the first time I felt very proud of myself. I knew my family was happy. Although Sam was ahead of me, his program took longer so he was going to graduate the following year for his undergraduate. That's the other reason why I couldn't have done medicine. It takes so much time of hard work. Not my cup of tea as I love fast tracks. I don't like too much complicated stuff. Not my way.

The day of graduation both my friends were also graduating and they also came with their families. Since we all came from the same neighbourhood, we planned to do our celebration together. All our families knew each other so they just agreed to our plan. Did they have much choice anyway?

The evening after the ceremony we all went to the banquet hall where we had our party. The three of us were picked up by a limousine together with our immediate families to the venue of the party. It was about six thirty in the evening when we all got to the venue and we were wearing our navy blue suits and light blue shirts and black bow ties. We were looking gorgeous. I know it's not the best to compliment yourself but on this one day I know for sure we had nailed it.

Soft music was heard playing from the back as we got inside. Cameras were seen flashing from all corners of the room as we walked past to greet our guests. We entered and went to sit at the VIP table. The banquet hall was beautifully decorated in blue and white. The colours almost matched our suits. The balloons were written, Congratulations Three Engineers, some, Congratulations Tim, Jimmy and Shelton.

I could see my father restless with joy and my mom trying to make sure that everyone was comfortable. It felt very good. After the greetings and all the people were settled, we went to the DJ and requested a song "Sorry" by Justin Bieber. In a few seconds all the younger people were in the middle of the dance floor. This was just at the beginning and so you could imagine what happened later.

The speeches took a bit of time since there were three families involved. We had asked our families to make it short but you know how it is with parents. My dad started his speech from since my childhood and honestly the most embarrassing moment was when he mentioned how I never wanted to shovel the snow. He said that I was born on the wrong sand. Everyone laughed before he gave the mic to the next speaker.

My auntie spoke in place of my mom and I could see the confusion when people glared at her. Those two looked alike. They were so identical that if you didn't know them personally you would just think it was one person. Their voices were the same as well. Very soft spoken. I remember when I was a little kid, it used to confuse me so much that the only way I could remember my mother was through the birthmark she had on the side of her cheek otherwise I wouldn't remember. To make matters worse, they both chose the same career. Both Registered Nurses.

I saw everyone's face looking at my auntie and then my mother just stood up and stood beside her.

"I can see that you are all confused..." my auntie started. "We both are Shelton Peters mothers." Laughter.

"Anyway I'm the twin sister to our graduate's mother. I'm her auntie from Calgary." All the people clapped in appreciation.

"I stand here today as Shelton's mother and I run short of words to see my son here graduating. I won't waste much of your time; I know everyone wants to enjoy. Just a few words to give to my son. To you Shelton, I want to tell you that this is now the beginning of real adulthood and you have to be wise in every decision you are going to make in the future."

The twin mothers hugged the new grads before they went to sit down. Speakers from the other two graduates also got up and gave their speeches which did not take much time as well.

The party continued until about three o'clock in the morning. Most people were very drunk and they were given rides by other guests and some took cabs home. Three o'clock is usually the time which the police do their patrols, so many people avoided risking. It was perfectly organized.

Chapter 3

Job Hunting

After graduation the hustle to look for work started. I was lucky to be hired at a local Shell company on a contract basis which lasted six months. For a novice like me, it wasn't bad and I was happy with my job.

My position was to cover for someone who had gone for maternity leave. The lady that I was replacing was supposed to be off for one year but ended up coming back only after six months. She stated that staying at home almost killed her. She couldn't stay home any longer. She said being home was boring and that's how she decided to cut her leave short. You know what that means; that's how I lost my first job.

Going back into job hunting was not easy at all. I was happy that at least my resume had some form of experience on it so here and there I got called for some temp jobs. I didn't have too much choice but I felt that, that was not what I went to school for. I needed something permanent and stable.

It was during the time when the economy in Alberta was booming. Jimmy and Tim heard there were great opportunities out there and they did not waste any time. I didn't want to hear anything about going out of the province, especially now that Shanna was away from home and I was the only one around my parents. I thought they would die.

I didn't want to think about it. I was just hoping and wishing to get something around the Greater Toronto Area. Time flew and nothing happened. I was just getting some short contracts and I can't count how many times I got laid off.

In this situation you can imagine the preaching of my dad. I remember one day when I was really down. I had just lost one job after two months and my father came to talk with me.

"Son you don't look alright. Is everything OK?"

I knew where his conversation was leading to, but oh God I couldn't avoid my old man.

"Yes dad, just that I'm concerned. I haven't gotten anything permanent ever since I graduated. It's about a year and half now and it's been bothering me a lot," I responded.

Dad came and sat beside me.

"I understand how you feel Shelton, but don't you think that maybe you chose a wrong career son?" He tried to pat my back and I resisted by shrugging my shoulders and screamed.

"There you go again dad. I knew you were going to say that. We should all be in the medical field, right? Father please, that's not fair. At least let me be."

I tried to calm down but I was still emotional.

"It's OK son. I'm sorry. I thought maybe..."

"That's fine dad, I know where you are coming from. I will just give myself a bit of time and see what happens."

"Sure son I will be on your back."

I was now starting to get very frustrated. Even though I was against the idea of moving up North like Tim and Jimmy, I was now at the early stages of depression. My mother noticed it and started to do some counselling and to give me some encouragement. I'm one person who had vowed never to move far away from my parents and also since I hated the long winters, I didn't want to try. It was the last thing that came into my mind at first until...

I lost a lot of weight in no time, I smoked more than I did before and I suffered insomnia. I felt worthless and like I wasted all my years in school for nothing. My friends also noticed that too through the conversations we had. Tim and Jimmy usually put me on a three-way conversation when they called.

"Hi Shelton, I think you should try to come here. I know you love Ontario so much and believe me man, we all do but you have to earn a living too."

It was Jimmy talking on the other end. I quietly listened on my S5 Galaxy phone which I had put on the Bluetooth.

"True to that. Shelton, just look at us here. We are all settled and you know at the oil fields where we are working they are looking for more engineers like yourself buddy. I believe if you submit your resume they can call you anytime soon. Just give it a try and if it doesn't work you can always go back. What do you think?" said Tim.

What could I think honestly? I was a jobless engineer, frustrated and getting all cooked up in my brains. After a long pause I then reluctantly answered.

"So what should I do now?"

"I would just suggest that you come here right away and I will talk to my manager. There are greater opportunities here and I know that they are looking for people now," Tim added.

"OK guys, thank you for your concern. I will think about it and let you know as soon as possible."

"Fine buddy think fast and let us know." We all hung up.

After a few days of weighing my options, I finally agreed to follow my friends. At first I was scared to tell my parents but ironically when I told them my idea they quickly agreed to it. My mother mentioned that she was also getting worried as well so this news was welcome.

At the end of two weeks I had landed in Fort McMurray, the oil sands. It was at the end of winter so it did not feel like much of a difference from Toronto. My friends rented an apartment in the city which they shared. We were all still bachelors so they just welcomed me and we lived together the same way we did when we attended Mohawk College.

They took my resume to their work places and in no time I was called for a job interview and was offered the job right away. I had never felt this relief like I did on this day in a long time. The job offer included a company car as well. To me that was a dream come true. I regret having wasted my time in Toronto. I had set my feet on the green pastures I had been looking for.

Fresh brains and more energy is how I felt at that point. I felt very revived, both my physical and mental being felt rejuvenated. My hope was resuscitated. I was now a new person. Engineer Shelton Peters. My confidence automatically came back.

Even though we stayed at the same apartment, the three of us could barely spend time together or see each other. Our schedules were different and usually when one was working days, one would be working night shift and we all worked at different sites although it was the same area. We usually just spoke on the phone or text.

My life was such a busy life. It was all work, work. We worked twelve hour shifts for twenty-one days and then seven days off. During my time off is when I would travel to Toronto to see my parents. At first I was traveling every month but my body started complaining. After twenty-one days of hard work sometimes you just need to take time to rest. So after a few months I started skipping one month and going home every other month and it worked out well and you know like expected, mom would start sending messages. Sometimes I would opt to visit my auntie in Calgary at least it was much better that way because it was closer.

In no time I started feeling like the man I have always wanted to be. I appreciated Jimmy and Tim very much and they teased me that I have to go to Ontario to enjoy my sunshine.

Chapter 4

My work

I worked at Suncor Oil sands with Jimmy whilst Tim worked at Shell sands, both in the same community but different sites.

I was quickly appointed to be a team leader and worked 12 hour rotating shifts of days and nights which I worked one week days and one nights alternatively. I was never used to working nights and I got startled easily during the day which would disrupt my sleep. During the first days I used to wake up after any little noise. It took no time before I adjusted to this new time table. The use of dark coloured curtains I put in my bedroom also helped to improve my sleep pattern during the day.

My job as a team leader included conducting test cell performance analysis for engine visits; drafting shop visit reports; supplying to customers within timeframe; troubleshooting engines in test cells; supporting training mechanics; and direct configuration control for power plant systems and components. In addition to that I also assessed test feed, boiler and service water, and managed emergency conditions.

It was a multitasking job which required body and mind to be together. After each shift we needed to take proper rest to re-boost our energy. I also managed log sheets and did temperature records so I did both physical and paper work. Accuracy was the key to all of this.

As usual, being a team leader required more dedication and commitment. You also needed to do your best and that was never my problem wherever I worked because I loved and enjoyed my work.

I also maintained the power plant and support maintenance personnel so you can imagine how demanding my job was. I was always all over the place most of the time. I also coached employees and administered equipment and work area. So all personnel especially the new hires would have to pass through me for training and safety handling programs like WHMIS.

Other duties that I had to do included power managing, process and thermopac boiler, control coal handling, ash conveying plant and also monitoring supplies delivery.

I must confess the people at the oil sands worked harder than any other places I have worked. The place is always busy and most people put extra hours all the time.

Sometimes it got tiring but like I said before, my body adjusted. Life at the oil sands was just basically work and home. There was nothing really interesting because by the time you finished work you just wanted to go to bed and sleep. Thank God they provide food for workers at the camps. I'm sure you would understand what it meant especially to bachelors like us. The only thing I loved doing after my long shift was sleeping and I rarely watched any TV shows.

My team usually involved fifty to eighty people. Most of the employees came from different provinces like Ontario, British Columbia and all other places. There were also people who came from out of the country as contractors.

From what I understood, most of the people from Ontario fell in the same category with me. They complained that they were getting frustrated with the unemployment rate. To those who were working, they still complained that they never got the jobs they were trained for especially the tradesmen. That was a valid reason. Those who lived in the neighbouring cities like Calgary and Edmonton usually came and lived in camps during working days and went home on off days. Some people were being flown in and out after their scheduled shifts.

Having accommodation at the camps was a great advantage to many workers since the accommodation in the communities around the area was high. People avoided incurring extra bills so most just took advantage of the services provided.

To those who knew how to save their money, this was a place to be. There wasn't a lot of things going on hence it was the best place to be if you wanted to save money.

For some time, I thought I was going to be there for a period until I sorted myself out. I meant until maybe when I raised enough cash to pay for a down payment for my house, but was that realistic? I never spent a lot of money on myself since I only had a few bills to pay. The only time I spent money was the time when I travelled home or when I spoiled my only sister Shanna. I actually had put her on a payroll that each time I got paid I would also send money to her. Although my brother Sam was still in school, he always told me that he was financially OK. I guess he was just playing a big brother thing. I knew Sam, he grew up a quiet person who never wanted to bother anyone. Not even me his one and only brother. I guess that's what he was trying to do. I didn't want him to work much since he had enough on his plate already with his studies so usually I would just deposit money into his account without him knowing.

My parents always told me that they were OK and never accepted any monetary gifts from me so I did force them to take. They surprised me one time when I rebelliously started putting money into their account and they later found out. It was my 25th birthday and like I always did; I went down south to celebrate with my family.

My dad now handed me a cheque of all the money I was depositing in their account. That was the day they gave me a big lecture of my life and like always, I just laughed it off. My dad told me that I should start investing and saving my money for better things in the future.

He went on telling me that the reason why my siblings and I never had to take any student loans was because they did plan wisely so he expected me to do way better than that. Sometimes I don't understand these old people. Dad said that they would only accept simple gifts like perfume and jewellery. Oh man you won't believe that he even gave me the names of the perfumes they liked. I knew my mom was sensitive with some scents because of her bad allergies so I understood where he was coming from.

Even though I was paying big attention to what he was saying I still felt it wasn't fair. Mom and dad were too organized for my liking. You won't believe this, just before I flew back to work they dragged me to the bank to meet with their financial advisor and you won't believe that I ended up opening accounts that I never planned to. Tax Free account, mutual funds...this. God you can never argue with these people and win.

When I got back to Fort McMurray and told my guys Jimmy and Tim about the craziness of my parents they all burst into laughter and Tim said that that's the reason he loved my dad. Really? I teased him that maybe we have to exchange parents and see if he would keep them and he said that he might not want to return them. We all laughed.

This was one of the few times that we all met and had some time to spend together. It happened once in three or four months and believe me we made sure that we made use of the time we had. Sometimes we went clubbing, and depending on the season, skiing or golfing and other activities.

Chapter 5

How I met my wife

There comes a time in a man's life when he starts feeling empty. When all material things mean nothing. I was now twenty-seven when all the dating I was doing was not fun anymore. Being in a place where you only have to worry only about work was no longer enjoyable. My parents started having a family when they were in their mid-twenties, that's why as we grew older we developed that friends-like relationship with them. My dad always said that he learnt some stuff from us.

It was those moments when we used to go golfing with father and when we played each other that were fun. You would take a lot of things for granted until when a time comes when all those things are not there anymore. No wonder why they said appreciate what you have when you still have it. It was now time that I started realizing how important my family was to me. Of course it was now practically impossible for us to be together again like living in the same house like we used to.

That feeling became more apparent when Tim announced that he was going to propose to his girlfriend, Lisa. The two had met at one of our outings at the club and from that day on Tim was never the same. It was love at first sight and they had automatically gotten glued to each other. When they were not working, it was rare to see Tim by himself unless if there was something very important. Lisa came from Edmonton and was also working as an administrator at one of the camp sites. She was living in the camps but since the establishment of this relationship she started spending more time at our apartment which we shared with Tim, so technically she had moved out of the camp.

Tim was my childhood friend since kindergarten so I was like a brother to him. I was very happy for the love bird's relationship but believe me, I started to feel a bit jealous of the two. Not that I wanted Lisa but each time I saw them together it made me feel lonelier. I was used to our boy times with Tim and suddenly someone appeared to have come between us. Believe me that's how I think Jimmy was feeling as well.

So this day when our best friend, our brother announced to us that he was going to propose, it was like a blow to us. I saw it in Jimmy's eyes as well. He looked at me for a moment without blinking and eyes wide open and I knew that we were on the same page.

From the way Tim sounded, it wasn't going to be long before the two walked down the aisle. Since it was winter time, they planned to have the wedding in the middle of the summer which was mid-July. We were all excited and we all got involved in the planning. I could tell that Tim had the dilemma of choosing between Jimmy and I who was going to be his best man for his wedding.

We discussed it and it could either be Jimmy or myself so I volunteered to be one of the groomsmen. I'm one person that is so uncomfortable with formal things so to sign a paper as a best man, oh no! That wasn't for me.

Jimmy had no problem with that so we voted him in. I like his carefree character though. Sometimes when we all felt uncomfortable to do certain things we would know that Jimmy would lead us. Funny, but I liked it. If not that Jimmy was mixed race, people would think that we were triplets. We had a strong bond.

For the groomsmen we were a team of seven including the best man. Most were Tim's cousins. It was a garden wedding which was held in Edmonton at the Lions Garden Centre. The deco was exquisite. The white and light teal cake matched the chair covers and the decorations. Everything translated beautifully from the cake to the table settings. It was a state of the art wedding.

The bridesmaids' dresses matched the decorations as well and our white suits also went with the ladies' shoes. Our flap pockets matched the girls' dresses. It was elegant.

The ceremony took place at the Catholic church which Lisa and her family attended and from there on we headed towards the photographs then we went to the venue for the party. It is one day I know that I got very drunk. I'm not usually a big drinker but at my best buddy's wedding I went above my normal limit. The biggest mistake I made was to mix beer with wine. After taking a few glasses of Pinot Gris white wine, my partner the bridesmaid offered me a green bottle, the Heineken. I was resistive at first because I had never mixed before but I was tempted to try. My brain was starting to sing a different song.

Stacy was one person who didn't care about her surroundings. She was the bride's best friend. I could tell that she was inebriated. I had lost control too. If I tell you that I remember what was taking place at that moment, I would be truly lying because I'm saying all this because I just put pieces together as I watched the video after the wedding. We got onto the dance floor and were on the stage by ourselves just the two of us. Everyone started cheering as we performed the song Lucy, by Destra.

You won't believe that I was that person that usually gets so anxious when it comes to going on stages. I think my parents were even shocked to see me dancing the way I did because even on my graduation day, if there was a way of sending someone to get my certificate from that stage I would have done so. I don't know where this sudden courage and confidence appeared from.

The party ended about three o'clock in the morning. I couldn't drive so I got into the car which was taking Stacy to her apartment.

The only thing that I remember very well is that I was surprised to see myself lying beside Stacy in her bedroom the following morning. I had this terrible headache and I wanted something to drink. I guess hangover was taking its toll. I noticed that I was still wearing my suit. Oh God! How did I get here? Stacy was still sleeping and I didn't want to disturb her so I made myself comfortable and found my way to the kitchen. Her apartment was a one bedroom so I didn't think otherwise, and besides she had told me that she was single.

After I helped myself with a drink I went into the living room and turned the TV on. That's when Stacy got up and joined me before she went to take a shower. My mouth was tasting yucky and all my toiletries were at the hotel room we were staying at. Fortunately, Stacy had some extra tooth brushes in her pantry.

Just when she left to the bathroom, I looked at the picture which was hanging on the wall in her living room. I must confess for the first time I felt something going on in my body. I saw how beautiful she was. Her tall slender figure sent some quick electrons into my brain. I stood up from the couch and got closer to the picture and I started having some goose bumps.

In a minute I had joined her in the tub and she started giving me a massage and vice versa. From then on one thing led to another and I later left to go and check out at the hotel after my parents called to tell me that they wanted to be dropped at the airport.

I had a week off so I wasn't in any hurry to go back to Fort McMurray. All I needed was to take my rest. I left to drop off my parents at the airport and promised Stacy that I would be back for dinner. I needed proper food. I knew at that point I had fallen for Stacy.

I had given my father my car the previous night so they picked me up and we went to the airport. I was happy that Stacy did not walk me downstairs because I was going to be embarrassed. I had told my family that we barely knew each other and if they saw that...

After dropping my family at the airport I decided to give Jimmy a quick call. I saw a lot of missed calls from him. I knew he was concerned because I did look awful the previous night. We chatted a bit and I gave him a quick update of the new developments with Stacy. He couldn't believe that I had fallen so quickly. That was really unusual of me. The people who know me well always told me that I was a picky monkey. True to that, but maybe I was also beginning to be mature or maybe I was changed by seeing my 'bestie' walking the aisle.

I didn't say that I was perfect, no. I also had times I did 'hitch hiking' like we used to call it. You may call it a one-night stand. The boys thing. Nothing serious and no attachment. So when I conveyed the news to Jimmy, at first he thought that it was our usual things. He told me that he was going to dig more information about this 'chick' from Lisa.

I heard him from the other end.

"I'm serious buddy. And guess what, this thing just happened and wasn't planned and I'm embarrassed to tell you that I didn't use any "CD." On my way back to the apartment I stopped by the Shoppers Drug Mart and went to Stacy's apartment. This time well prepared.

I ended up spending my whole week at her place before I went back to Fort McMurray. From then on, the relationship got stronger and what we started as just a fling was now leading somewhere.

Chapter 6

Marriage proposal

You know that feeling when you know you have found the person you want to spend the rest of your life with, your heart tells you right away. I used to believe that you have to date for years before you decide to settle down. I couldn't believe myself when I told Jimmy and Tim that I didn't need to have a Bachelors degree of studying Stacy before I proposed to her.

The writing was on the wall that this man was now considering taking the next step in the relationship. After dating for three months I invited Stacy to come with me down South to Toronto to formally meet my family. My auntie from Calgary also flew down with us although she got a direct flight.

Stacy's family all lived in Edmonton and I had been to their place a couple of times already. Its 'kinder cool' to be accepted by the family of your potential future wife. Stacy worked Monday to Friday so her schedule allowed her to come to Fort McMurray every Friday and I would also travel to Edmonton during my off days.

I felt that I didn't need to waste more time before I settled down. At first I thought it was going to be tough for me to convince my family that I had finally found the love of my life but to my surprise they all stated that they had felt the connection with her at Tim's wedding. It is just a normal feeling that most people want to get those blessings from the ones they love. It's just a special feeling.

I knew mom had approved of her when she quickly said we should come home. I'm sure her twin sister must have told her great things about Stacy when we visited her because after we left Calgary to introduce her she called me and was sounding very excited. I don't know what she liked about her that she saw in that short time we were there.

Some of her comments were, "she seems genuine, she is real, and she speaks her mind out." I remember after she finished talking that I asked her, "Is that all you saw in her?" She went on saying she was just going to talk to my mother and that she knew I couldn't get any better than her. We all laughed and hung up.

By the time I told mom and dad that I was going to bring the girl they saw at the wedding, they were already fully detailed about her so they just expressed how much they had been waiting for this.

Stacy was concerned about her behaviour at the wedding. She thought maybe they were going to judge her according to that. She knew that we had gone wild, you know after a couple of beers on a very hot summer day. I kept on telling her that my parents were the kind of people who didn't care much about petty issues. They always told us that what we were doing now, they have also done it in their time so it didn't bother them much. All they cared for was our happiness and that's what they said mattered most.

We couldn't get a direct flight from Edmonton so we went through Winnipeg. We finally got home at about seven o'clock in the evening because of the long stay over at the Richardson International Airport. Stacy was sleepy most of the time and I thought that maybe she was over exhausted. She hadn't eaten anything since morning and wasn't really looking herself. She looked more worn out.

When we got to Richardson International Airport, I asked her if she wanted to have something to eat and she said she wasn't that hungry and I thought it was one of those feelings when one is going to meet the future in laws. I forcibly bought her a cheese burger with tomato from True Burger which was usually her favourite. She took a bite and I saw her frowning her face and she quickly rushed to the bathroom. She told me that she was sick in the stomach which got me worried. I quickly sent a message to my mother as I felt very helpless.

Mother called back and told me to get her checked out since we still had a lot of time. I googled the address of the nearest Walk in Clinic and it was not far from the Airport that we could just use a cab to get there. I then shared my mom's idea with my sweetheart and she refused to go. She told me that it was nothing serious. I felt so helpless and then after sometime she told me that she had news to share with me. My heart jumped out. My epinephrine went up. I could only think of the worst. My mind rushed everywhere.

After moments of silence she noticed that I had become very restless when she asked me to pass her, her handbag which was on the floor. I slowly picked it up, opened the zipper and held it patiently for her to get what she wanted. I thought maybe there were some medications she was taking that I didn't know of. Surprisingly she pulled out a white folded paper and handed it to me.

I dropped the handbag down, my attention driven to what she was handing to me. My eyes on the paper and, "Oh my Go...pregnancy test positive."

I screamed and jumped from my chair until she stood up and reminded me that we were still at the airport.

"I'm going to be a father..."

The poor girl was feeling ashamed. After some moments, I finally sat down, hugged and kissed her and asked her why she kept this away from me.

"I just got the results yesterday and I thought you would be overwhelmed so I planned to tell you when we get to Toronto."

I quickly called my mother. That was the greatest news in my life. I felt connected to Stacy more than before. Tears of joy were showing in my eyes. I started feeling like a family man. We then started talking about the baby, like she was already there. We then connected to our flight home and when we got to the airport all my family members and the extended family were there. They were holding balloons written 'Welcome home' and some flowers. We got into Sam's car home.

When we got home I was surprised to see the house full. My grandparents were all there and all my cousins and their families. It was like a mini wedding. That's one thing I know about my parents. Very traditional. Sometimes the things they do I wonder if they are even necessary and they always have a perfect reason to suit the situation.

Everyone already knew that Stacy was pregnant and they were trying to be very cautious with her. My grandfather, mom's dad, who we call Pastor

Papa also came to the airport to pick us up. He is known for his charming and compassionate personality. He always does everything to his best.

On our way home, we showed Stacy the schools that I attended. It was her first time to visit Ontario so she was comparing and admiring places.

 When we got home, grandpa Pastor prayed and welcomed us. My two mothers were busy pampering my soon to be wife. I felt so humbled. Mom called me privately and reminded me how she always said we should not take advantage of anyone. She was overjoyed and so she already gave me her blessings.

That weekend we were busy and we just decided that we were going to get married. Everyone pledged to help and it appeared like we planned the wedding in one day. I felt so honoured. I didn't think my family was going to be of much support to us. Stacy too was overwhelmed by the way everyone welcomed her.

On Sunday when most people had left we decided to go and visit Niagara Falls since Stacy had not been there. It was soothing walking at the falls with the person I loved. We spent the whole day there and by the time we went back home, we were so exhausted and we got ready for our morning flight.

Chapter 7

Starting a family

We tried to rush things before the baby bump became too big. A marriage date was set to be held within three months. Everything went smoothly and after three months we were officially Mr. and Mrs. Peters. What a joy.

Our marriage minister was my grandpa pastor and it was my best moment in life. His words to us were that if we were ever to get divorced, it means that we were going to break a record in history since all the marriages he blessed were still standing. Strong words indeed. I couldn't hold my tears.

After our honeymoon we went back to Fort McMurray and now looking forward to an additional family member. Stacy was now in her third trimester and was now looking heavily pregnant. That's when we thought that it was time we needed a bigger place.

We went to the bank and our mortgage was approved right away. We started looking for a house and we finally agreed on buying in the Beacon Hill neighbourhood, the same neighbourhood with Tim and Lisa. Our houses were just one street apart. We moved in just about a month to Stacy's due date. It was a three-bedroom house with a finished basement. It was a beautiful home especially for a young family; there was enough space for the kids to play at the backyard.

The house was a few years old and it didn't need much work except for paint. I needed to change the colour otherwise it was perfect and to what we expected.

We fixed the baby's room and I managed to furnish it before the baby came. Since we already knew the sex of the baby, we painted her room pink and it was all nicely decorated in no time.

Baby was born at the Northern Heights Regional Health Centre. I was there to cut the umbilical cord and it was such an amazing feeling to hold my first baby.

My mom had flown from Toronto to come and see her first grandchild. Stacy's mom came after the baby was born.

We now had two babies in the house. My little poodle was spoiled so now we had to divide the attention. His name was Ricky. Ricky was one of the most adorable dogs you could ever wish to have. I loved him. The first days when he saw Stacy, he used to feel jealous seeing us together. He used to bark and always wanted to sit between us until after he felt less intimidated.

So the when Tracy, our baby came, Ricky would always come and sit watchfully beside her. Very much protective indeed. I felt very fulfilled having my beautiful family. Stacy also suggested we adopt a cat so we now had a dog, a cat and Tracy.

We did not waste much time after Tracy was born so we quickly planned to have a second baby just when Tracy turned one. We have always wanted our children to grow up together and we weren't getting any younger as well.

It felt fulfilling. We were happy and content with what we had. Working at the oil sands was such a rewarding thing. Financially we were very much satisfied.

As time went by, a lot of people started flocking into Fort McMurray and we felt that it was a good investment if we put our resources into another house. It sounded like an idea to my wife who agreed at once. That's how we bought our second property and we rented it out. The house was in the same neighbourhood that we lived in. Getting some tenants at that point was not a big issue because of the population growth in the city. With the demand of oil, the market went high and there were a lot of employment opportunities that had attracted many people.

Some workers were coming from different provinces and some came from outside of the country. I remember during one of my training sessions with my new hires and during our discussions, most mentioned that they were attracted by the idea of having long term opportunities offered by Fort McMurray and the high wages as compared to other provinces. It was ideal for people who lived in the camps since the cost of living had gone so high. Accommodation was not as cheap compared to other places away from the oil sands. When the demand increased, the prices hiked as well. It was so with the houses. As the population grew, the prices went up as well. Surprisingly even with those high prices, people were still buying.

Chapter 8

Recession

All went well for most people until the beginning of 2015 when the booming economy of the oil sands crashed. In fact, it was noted to have affected the whole province when Alberta went into a big recession.

The price of oil was noted to have gone down in the international market which affected the production hence most companies were left with no choice other than to shelve the new projects since they were no longer profitable. It was very sad when people started losing their jobs.

It was a very stressful moment to see that most of the people I was working with were being laid off. I was lucky that I survived but still hurting to see some of the people going home. The most difficult thing was for me to hand the laying off letters to my staff. My heart was broken. There are times in life when you have to stop thinking about yourself and start thinking of others.

Some people, especially from out of the country and other provinces just dumped their cars and left. Most were still on credit. The situation was very bad; you wouldn't know if you are the next to be sent packing. That's what almost killed me. The fear of the unknown.

My family referred to me as a weak person. I must say that I agreed with them at that point. There were a lot of other people who had more seniority than me at work and that left me just hanging in the air. I thought my chances were very slim. This uncertainty of the future changed us to be different people. We started cutting off a lot of things on our budgets.

The people who rented our other house were also laid off and that practically left us with two mortgages. We thought of different options and one option was to sell the house but the reality was that there was no one to sell the house to.

I'm not the only person who suffered in this situation as most people had also acquired second properties. That's the time I regret why I didn't invest in some other places. I know my dad had told me to buy my second property in Toronto. He said the housing market was also booming and I believed in myself. Life at that point was going the direction I wanted in Fort McMurray. No wonder they say don't put all your eggs in one basket. I felt it this time around.

We finally got some other new tenants who of course were going to pay way less rent. It was still better than nothing and all we wanted was to have someone to keep the house. Some apartments became empty and very cheap as well. I know the apartment we used to rent with my "besties" went down a lot. The rent was slashed by 1/3. That's how suffocating this situation was.

Talking of the house prices in terms of buying, all houses went into negative equity. For example, when we bought our house, it was at a higher price due to the demand, and if we were to sell it now, it would sell for less than what we bought it for and we would still be owing the bank.

It wasn't fun at all. That's the time I learnt to spend and also save some on the side. Fort McMurray's wages were much higher than most provinces. As much as we can testify that, the surprising thing was, most did not have any savings when the recession attacked.

I had a colleague at work who gave up his house because he couldn't cope with the mortgage payment. He went into a depression so severe that at one point he was admitted at the mental hospital. He couldn't cope with the change, and it was really a big change so I did understand him. Dealing with stress is hard. All the people around him tried to encourage him but all didn't make sense to him.

Not only he was affected with this whole change. From what I saw on the news, some people had already committed suicide because they couldn't handle this. Coping with bills is always hard even when you have a job and it becomes worse when you only have to live on employment insurance.

I survived that recession but I was psychologically affected. You get connected to the people you work with and what affects them affects you. So it was with me with this recession.

Chapter 9

The Blaze

I was sitting in the lounge watching TV on the night of May the 1st 2016, when I saw that there was a wildfire which was noted to have started at the Southwest of Fort McMurray in Alberta. To me it was one of those fires which always start and it would stop.

I called Stacy, who was busy putting the kids to bed and shared the news. She also responded that it was the usual thing during that season. She went on saying that whatever happens we know that the fire fighters would always win the fire. Stacy is one person who always stays positive so whatever happens she would quickly find a positive answer to it.

I think that's one of her characteristics that I loved about her. I remember during the time when the recession started, she would always have something positive to say and always came with all the possible ways we would live our life in case I did lose my job. Not to brag about my wife or because I love her but she is just one of the most amazing people I have ever met. Thinking of it, before I left Toronto, I had already gotten so depressed that my family was even worried, but there came someone who always sees every positive thing out of any storm.

As I continued watching the news Tim and Jimmy called and we were on three-way. Our usual thing. We discussed how we were all lucky to have survived the recession. The best thing was that all of us survived it. It would not have been good on my part if any one of them had gotten laid off because my buddies had brought me here. I would feel bad. We then had other discussions like the basketball playoffs.

As usual the following day, which was the Monday, I went to work and still following on the news, I saw that the fire was growing even bigger. When I got up Tuesday morning, I saw that the wildfires had prompted evacuation orders for residents of Prairie Creek and Centennial Trailer Park and that alerts were in place for other areas. They warned that the fire outside Fort McMurray had doubled in size by Monday evening and they were concerned that the weather conditions would pose a great challenge.

As usual, the Tuesday morning we all got up and went to work and dropped our kids at school on our way. My six-year-old girl Tracy doing grade one and my four-year-old son in junior kindergarten both attended the school located in our neighbourhood, very close to our house so it was very easy to pick and drop them. Stacy now worked downtown where she worked with the City Council.

I was just about to finish my lunch break when she called. Her voice sounded very shaky and disturbed.

"Honey we are supposed to get out of the city right now...Fire."

For a moment I was stunned. My mind rushed to our house. I completely forgot about the wildfire.

"What? What happened? Where are you?" I was firing questions to her without giving her any chance to answer.

"OK, Shelton calm down, the wildfire is said to be coming towards this direction and as it is everyone is supposed to be getting out for Edmonton."

I now had a picture of what was going on.

My work was quite a distance from the city. So we had to think and act fast.

"OK so you go get the kids. I will go home and pick the stuff we need OK."

"Great I think that works, let me rush to school and pick them up."

"Great."

I told everyone at work and in panic and rush, everyone rushed to their cars. In no time the roads were packed. Just driving to the city was the most stressful thing ever and I kept checking my wife if she had managed to get the kids from school. I was happy when she said she had already picked them up and she was already heading towards highway 63 which goes to Edmonton. The traffic was now moving very slow and roads were packed.

Just when the evacuation order was given, everyone started calling all the people they knew so communication was really excellent. Even the ones who did not know each other, people were just knocking on doors to make sure that everyone was out.

My mind rushed to Ricky and Bentley my cat. I couldn't imagine what was happening to them. The scariest thing was that they announced that the speed of the wind which blew the fire towards the city kept on increasing. When things are not moving at the pace you want, you feel very stressed. This was with me when the traffic wasn't moving. I called Stacy and she told me the stuff she wanted me to bring especially for the kids.

Time was moving and updates on the news were saying the fire was almost reaching the city. In fact, you didn't need to be told that because the sky was looking cloudy with smoke. The blaze which was some few kilometres away seemed to be getting closer. The smoke which the fire produced was now coming into my nostrils and I could imagine my poor baby Tracy who was asthmatic.

She struggles in winter and with this, oh Go...I called Stacy right away to remind her not to open the windows. We were already in a difficult situation as it was and to add petrol to fire my baby was highly allergic and sensitive to a lot of things. I was very concerned. I wanted to get home and pick up her drugs. In fact, that was one of the main reasons to go home and of course to get Ricky and Bentley out.

My heart was bleeding. It was now getting very dark like it was night time but it was not even four o'clock in the evening. Had it not been for my cat and my dog, I could have made a U-turn and gone to the highway. The closer I got home, the scarier it became. My heart was divided but I thought I couldn't let my cat and dog die and we didn't know when we would come back.

I was crying when I got home. I parked my car on the side of the road. Just when I got out of the car I saw a big flame behind my big house. I then tried to get to open the door when suddenly I heard a loud voice.

"Run...Ruuuuu...n!"

I looked behind and I saw a guy screaming and I rushed towards them.

"Oh my God. My house…"

There was no chance for me to even get into the car. I was numb for a moment as I watched the fire growing from my house roof.

It was like watching a Tom Cruise movie with everything happening so fast. I only woke up from this dream when I was dragged by the shoulders by a good Samaritan into his car.

"We have to go buddy."

I couldn't believe what I was seeing. My car I just parked was already in flames within a space of minutes. A flood of tears was running down my cheeks. Words failed me. We were almost getting out of Beacon Hill when the fire continued to double coming towards our direction. We were now in the good Samaritan's car.

At first we were given directions to go downtown where we spent much time roaming up and down. We were meant to believe that downtown was safer.

In no time the directions had changed and we were supposed to be out. We headed towards highway 63. I was worried about my family. My wife and kids were in the convoy but no communication. My cell phone was in the car which caught fire. I knew for sure by then Stacy was also worried about my whereabouts. It never rains but it pours. Just when we wanted to head towards the highway, the gas tank went red. The car stopped.

We did not waste time. We just got out of the car, dumped it there and jumped into one car which was also on the convoy. No one asked or said anything. It was like we were obligated to be there. Life is just not predictable. We started going slowly onto the highway. The traffic was now being directed towards one direction so it did help a bit but still the jam was too much.

All evacuees were very cooperative. Since we started getting out of the city, we started seeing lots of cars left on the side of the roads. We just assumed they had the same gas problems we also had.

No one really talked only eyes were looking and crying. Just when we were about to get out of the city or at the entrance of Fort McMurray from Edmonton, we saw a hotel, Super 8, on fire. The wind was now blowing more than before. The fire had now crossed the road and had started burning the other side of the road.

The heat even in the car was becoming too much and we couldn't open windows. I felt sorry for the driver and I just uttered words that if he felt tired of driving we could help. My mind stopped thinking for a bit. I was hoping to wake up from this dreadful longest nightmare. I had never in my entire life experienced such a hard life. It felt like a hard pinch of a soft skin.

We introduced ourselves about three and a half hours after we got into the stranger's car. It was after we had passed the burning hotel. The guy driving told us that he worked at the hotel that was burning. He was crying.

I told them that my family was ahead and there was no communication whatsoever since my phone was burnt in the car. He then offered me his cell phone to use to call and check on them.

I didn't want to tell my wife a lot of things because she would just panic and driving with kids. I just told her that I was fine and was in traffic and that I had misplaced my phone. I just had to come up with a story. What doesn't kill you makes you stronger. It was the same in this case, it had to be. Man don't cry...

I tried to be as strong as I could. I guess all the people did. Our eyes were all red. The smoke became more apparent and the sky looked thick like the Nimbostratus before heavy rains. I was shaking. I didn't know if we were going to survive this and live to tell a story. The first good Samaritan who had dragged me from my house stated that he also lived in the same neighbourhood that I lived. He mentioned that he had only managed to come out with some important documents.

The Dodge Caravan we were in had three people in it and still the car was very full. This guy was one of the lucky people who managed to pack some stuff. He said that when he heard the announcement, he started packing thinking that he still had enough time. He regrets that he had wasted his time doing that. By now he would have been out of this whole mess. I also told him that all I had was now history. All gone........

I lost control of myself and started crying. We tried to comfort one another as we all didn't know the outcome of this situation. We were all sailing in the same boat. The traffic was going at just above 1 km per hour.

Now the traffic was ordered to go the same direction and you would think that would help but believe me, that's when I saw how big my community was. As we continued going, we also saw the togetherness of my community. No one was left stranded. With the number of cars left at the edges of the roads, you would think that some people would be stuck. People just helped each other and most cars were overloaded.

As we continued talking, the driver stated that his sister who worked at the hospital had told him that all the patients were evacuated safely. Her husband had to pick the children while she had to stay at work. I started to appreciate service people more. They put other people first yet they also have their own families. As it was, the fire had gone out of control and the fire fighters were trying to do all they could...I learnt to appreciate more. Their lives were at stake as well. I started looking at life in a different way.

The worst part of all this was when we saw a Shell gas station burning. We thought we had seen the worst when we saw the hotel going down but this was so distressing. The driver was really strong otherwise he would have lost it. The fire was big and you know how gas stations are beside the roads especially on highways, the fire was getting very strong towards the roads. People were honking at each other as they wanted to pass. Everyone wanted to pass this as soon as they could but it was practically impossible.

The flame continued to grow bigger and stronger. The smoke now covered the area like a dark cloud. Our driver, now very much stressed started shouting "God help us please...God!"

We both held hands and started praying. As the wind continued to blow, fire particles also blew to the road. It became scarier. We started to see some fire trucks coming. Police sirens were also heard following behind. That put all the vehicles on standstill.

Most people turned off their vehicles for some time as they didn't want to waste gas for nothing. Our driver followed suit. He also wanted to stretch a bit but there was not much space. My body was getting cramps as well. After some time, the traffic slowly started moving. It was a great relief to both of us. I was now feeling very thirsty. It was very dry in the car. We were lucky because the driver Steve, the owner of the car had a bottle of water which we all shared. I couldn't imagine those people who struggled to get even a drink of water. I appreciated a lot of things on this day.

The happiest moment of all this was when we got to Fort McKay, which is about fifty kilometres from Fort McMurray. We saw a Petrol gas station which was open and the line was just unbearable. It looked like every car needed a fill up. We all jumped out of the car and rushed to find washrooms. The line itself was also big and a lot of us went to relieve ourselves in the bush.

I was lucky to find a wallet on me because usually when I'm driving I just put it in the car, which at this point must have been ashes. I got orders from the others so we could get something to eat. By the time we managed to get in, all the food stuffs were almost running out. People were buying more because of fear of the unknown.

It took us more than two hours just standing in line before we got served. It was ridiculous. We finally managed to get bread and some pop. We all sat down and ate. It was now past midnight then. I had to check on my wife who told me that she was almost in Edmonton. I was happy and didn't have to worry much about them at this moment. After stretching a bit, we got back into the car and proceeded.

The highway was still packed. It looked like it was now worse than it was before. Traffic wasn't moving that much. After travelling for a few kilometres we decided to park on the side of the road and sleep. We needed a break. We were exhausted. We woke up at seven o'clock in the morning and proceeded. We finally got into Edmonton at about three o'clock in the afternoon. This was the longest time I had ever spent traveling by road.

Chapter 10

Arriving in Edmonton

When they saw me coming out of a stranger's car, they automatically knew what it was. It was all over the news and they had more updates than we did. All our neighbourhood was gone. Ashes. History. When you see everything that you have ever earned burning down, it's just unbearable.

We all got into my mother in law's house and tears were all over. We hugged and cried. My mother in law offered to host all of us for the night.

My heart was broken. I was hurt inside and out. What ate me most was the fact that I wasn't able to save the poor souls. My Ricky and Bentley. I had had Ricky ever since I moved to Fort McMurray and he was so much attached to me. He was my first baby before I got married. We used to go for joy rides together and he was very much spoiled. I had bought him at the local pet shop when he was newly born and I had had him for about eight years now.

To me my Ricky was not just an ordinary dog. He knew when I was sad and he would come and sit on my lap as to comfort me. He knew when I was happy and he was always a contribution to my joy. He was like my alarm to remind me to wake up in case I overslept when I had to go to work. Until I got married, he would come and sleep in my bedroom, and sometimes on my bed. We were so much attached, that's why when Stacy came into the picture, Ricky was sad. He thought someone had stolen his position. That was my story with Ricky. May his dear soul rest in peace. I will miss him.

Talking about Bentley, oh God... I knew for sure it was going to be very difficult for my poor kids. They loved him so much and he was always watching over them especially when they were babies. He always slept in either of their bedrooms. My kids loved to take care of him so it was their responsibility to feed him. It was their choice and we had given them the opportunity to fulfil their wish.

Animals are fun sometimes. Bentley would sense if the two kids were fighting to play with him. He would then make sure that he goes to them at different times and make sure he shared his time with each one of them.

It was hard for everyone. Our houses and the car were gone. I had completely lost control over everything and had become a spectator of my life. Nothing was making any sense.

My sister in law had left the house and came back after an hour. I thought she had gone back to her house since she also lived in the neighbourhood, close to my parents in law, when she came back. We were all sitting in the lounge when we heard a doorbell ring. My sister in law came back and with a smile on her face she stated that she had a surprise for us. She wasn't holding anything so we all wondered what the surprise was.

As we continued looking, we saw my mom and dad walking in. We hugged and cried for some time.

After we all calmed down my mother started talking.

"I know this is not easy for you my children, but thank God you are alive. We have you here now. It could have been worse."

Words were difficult coming out of her mouth. My dad who had been quiet all this time also added.

"True, I couldn't imagine what the worse could be like, and remember son, when you came from Ontario, I remember you only had two bags and now you are talking of houses. You can always get these material things but you can never put any value to life. We have all of you here, you have yourselves, your life. That's all that matters. Thank God that so far we haven't heard any fatalities through this fire."

Powerful words indeed. We all hugged again. Tears falling down but this time the burden less heavy.

"Yes we do have each other." We all shouted with joy.

There is always something positive out of every negative situation. We are alive. That's all that matters.

Chapter 11

Appreciation

As we continued watching the news, we saw that there were places which were offering food and shelters open to accommodate people. The support we got was really amazing. Some shops put some discounts for clothing items. It did make a big impact on us since most people had left their houses with nothing.

The community of Edmonton was just unbelievable. Some people offered accommodation. It was so amazing the kind of love and support we received. Some newcomers like the Syrian refugees came out to help. They put money together and believe me nothing is too small. Some restaurants offered food etc. This is to mention but a few.

Talking about the Government of Canada, the Red Cross, the Salvation Army and other organizations, we can't thank them enough for the sleepless nights spent trying to make us comfortable. Our fire fighters and the outside Canada support, you are true heroes. We do salute you.

We also do appreciate the great communication within the community. It could have been worse.

Whilst I'm telling my story, I'm in the comfort of knowing that Fort McMurray will stand again. It will function to its maximum capacity and we know how hard we work. Let's not allow the blaze that destroyed my shadow to destroy our abilities.

Chapter 12

Conclusion

Having said all that, I was awakened by the noise of my mother's prayer who was sitting beside me. My wife stated that I had been hallucinating all night. This was the first night I had put my body down to really relax after coming out of the blaze. My wife was sitting beside the bed and from the way it looked, they must have been there for a while. I don't know what I was saying but I know that I took a long time before I eventually fell asleep.

My mind was racing everywhere. I was thinking of how our children were going to adjust from that comfort life they were used to. Change on its own is always a challenge to everyone and talking of the kids, I felt it was going to hit them badly even though at this point they seemed fine. They might have been still in shock themselves. Even though the insurance would help us to rebuild our homes and go back, will it ever be the same again? There are always those special things you have that can never be replaced by money. Those special toys bought on birthdays and those nice memorable pictures. How would my children adjust to all that? How about the school? How long would it take before they rebuild? Everything in their lives was going to change. When I thought of Ricky and

Bentley my heart started to bleed. I thought if it was not easy for me as an adult, how were my children going to take it? A lot of counselling was going to be needed.

I also thought of the hustle it was going to be to go from office to office trying to recover the lost documents. Birth certificates, health cards, everything, you name it, was all gone. How were we going to manage that stress? Thank God we are living in the world of technology. I know we are guaranteed that all our information will be stored, otherwise it would be bad. I hate standing in lines, even those short moments that I go and stand for my licence plates, I always feel like the line is too long. Let me put it this way, I'm not a very patient person.

Another thing that raced into my mind was the way I looked into my life. I saw that I was living in the illusion of seeing myself as an engineer who had achieved this and that. My life was all focused and based on my homes. All the material things that I had acquired. All those material things that I was praising myself for were now my shadow that was destroyed by the blaze.

The blaze was just a one-day tragedy which destroyed all the things built over the years. Just in one day. This changed my perception on life. The fire might have destroyed all that we had but those powerful words which my parents had said made me a new being. Just being alive, was enough to be thankful. Instead of crying for what we have lost, we should start cherishing what we have. Just being here around my family was worthwhile. It could have been worse.

I was hit with guilt when I thought of the other time I was watching TV when I saw the floods and the mudslides in the Philippines. I just treated it as ordinary news. After having gone through this, my heart went to humanity. Have I gone out of my way for others or do I always think about myself only? You won't understand what guilt does to a person. I felt I had not done enough for others. My eyes just became open that we should love one another and always care for the ones in need.

From the moment I was dragged from the fire at my house by the good Samaritan, I saw love. Now as I put my head down, my mind racing everywhere, I went deeper down my memory lane trying to understand and appreciate what I have gained through this experience. The way we jumped into Steve's car as if we knew him...it just made me cry. The new person I saw myself is a person who is full of love, the one who will also get out of his own comfort zone for others. Steve's car was full but he did not look at that, he just let us squeeze in. That's humanity. Some people learn through circumstances.

I know I love my family so much, but until this situation, I didn't realize how much it means to have the ones you love around you, especially when you are facing a challenge. Having the support of my whole entire family made the burden bearable. I had shoulders to cry on. From the time we got to Edmonton, my parents in law were busy on their feet trying to make us comfortable. Their neighbours also came, some brought food and other stuff like clothing. I never would have thought of going an extra mile for anyone but this had opened my eyes big time.

You might not understand this if you haven't faced any challenge before like I did but after having gone through this, the love I saw was just amazing. I'm convicted with guilt of not having given to others. I always thought about myself only but now I'm changed. The blaze might have destroyed my illusion but I have gained humanity.

The End